# Around Leek

## IN OLD PHOTOGRAPHS

A late Victorian photograph of Derby Street.

# Around Leek

## IN OLD PHOTOGRAPHS

### RAY POOLE

Alan Sutton Publishing Limited
Phoenix Mill · Far Thrupp · Stroud
Gloucestershire

First Published 1994

Copyright © Ray Poole, 1994

**British Library Cataloguing in Publication Data.**
A catalogue record for this book is available from
the British Library.

ISBN 0-7509-0623-5

Typeset in 9/10 Sabon.
Typesetting and origination by
Alan Sutton Publishing Limited.
Printed in Great Britain by
The Guernsey Press Company Limited,
Guernsey, Channel Islands.

A typical Leek 'millscape' viewed from Park Road. Clemesha Brothers and Birch Ltd,
Spilsbury's Dyeworks and California Mill all cluster around the rows of workers'
houses in Horton Street while the Nicholson Institute dominates the skyline. Built in
1884 to the design of the Leek architects William and Larner Sugden, the building is a
fine example of Leek's splendid Victorian architecture.

# Contents

This splendid character study of a local Edwardian gentleman is typical of the family portraits so popular at the time. The photograph was taken by J. Rider, King Street. Studios such as this were equipped with elaborate and often exotic backgrounds, against which the elegantly dressed subject posed proudly. It perfectly captures the spirit of a vanished age, which this book seeks to reflect.

# Introduction

Leek can rightly be described as the town that silk built. Early documents and inventories show that the seeds of the silk industry were sown in the seventeenth century, nurtured by the early button men and cottage weavers, and reached full bloom in the Victorian era.

These were Leek's 'golden years' when the industry grew and prospered, and the town developed commercially and economically. The population increased steadily as mounting numbers of people found employment in the mills, giving rise to a demand for housing – a demand that was met by the proliferation of streets of good standard terraced properties. Streets of uniform terraces, some with weavers' attic 'shades' in the upper storey, interlaced with cobbled passages between the houses, form a typical mill town scene in several parts of the town. In this way, Leek has a great affinity with the hard, gritty northern Pennine industrial towns, and should resist any misguided planning attempts to make it a 'garden suburb' – which it certainly is not!

The wealth created by the textile industry enabled Leek to exploit all the fashionable trends in Victorian architecture, art and design, as the generosity of the mill owners endowed the town with a rich heritage of fine Victorian buildings – a townscape of a style, scale and quality usually found in much larger conurbations. Many of Leek's factories, far from being in the 'dark satanic mills' style, were built with a great deal of imagination and flair, and remain today as fine examples of the best in Victorian architecture. The work of the local architects, William and Larner Sugden, is supreme in this field, and the influence of the Arts and Crafts movement, with its William Morris associations, can be seen in many of Leek's buildings.

Coincident with the development of the textile industry there has remained, permanent and enduring, the status of Leek as a market town. Awarded its Market Charter in 1208, in the reign of King John, Leek has held its position as the focal point of the local agricultural community for hundreds of years.

Leek's title of 'Queen of the Moorlands' aptly reflects its unique status within the Staffordshire moorlands, where farming conditions range from the wild, windswept and treeless high moors, where the grouse has its home and the sheep roam free, to the more temperate and gentle well-watered green valleys, where cattle and arable farming are well established in farmsteads that have often been owned by the same family for many generations.

In town and village, the Staffordshire moorlands are an area of great contrasts, and the changing pattern of life in the area is reflected in the pages which follow. Leek has been fortunate to have a number of local photographers who have recorded the passing scene. W.H. Nithsdale, George Hill and W.H. Horne spring readily to mind, and their work is well represented, coupled with the more commercial postcard photographs, and much work of unknown origin.

But a district is much more than its commerce, its industries and its buildings – it is people who give any town its human face. Personalities and human activities put flesh on the bare bones of history, and Leek has never been short of 'characters' and events. The usual generic term for the people of Leek is not 'Leekites' but 'Leekensians', which has a much better ring. This book is therefore dedicated to all Leekensians, past and present.

So, my dear Leekensian, you may well find yourself within these pages, for we are concerned with people rather than buildings, and you are ageless and timeless. You have been a pupil in Leek's schools, you have worked in its silk mills, you have attended its weekly market and traded in its fine old shops. You have walked in its processions and seen its soldiers off to war. You have applauded its royal visitors and sung in its choirs. You have travelled its wild moorland tracts and sat beside its tranquil waters. You have endured its bitter winters, and enjoyed its fine summers, with their old-established traditions.

In short, you are a thread in the intricate pattern of Leek and the moorlands, which, like the multicoloured silks woven into the fabrics for which Leek is so famous, takes its place as part of the pattern as a whole. You are therefore a vital part of this rich history, and when you realize this the past takes on an immediacy with the present, history lies all around you, and the continuing process of history has the nearness of yesterday.

This elaborate souvenir commemorating the marriage of Mr and Mrs Arthur Nicholson was printed in colour on a high quality card. It shows an artist's impression of the firm's various factory buildings, though not necessarily in their correct places, and is an indication of the flair and quality which Leek's Victorians brought to their activities.

# The Happiest Days of Your Life

The little school in Pump Street, off Ball Haye Green, was built in 1871 to cater for 164 children. That part of the town was then separate from the main town of Leek – a community in its own right. St Luke's was a church school and the teacher at this time was Miss Spinks. She was later followed by Mr Joseph William Swift. When this picture was taken in about 1912 the headmaster was Mr Charles M. Bell.

W.H. Nithsdale took this photograph in about 1904. He has captured the joyous freedom of these country children skipping happily home from the old Ramshaw Primary School, on the Buxton Road just beyond Ramshaw Rocks.

All Saints' School, grade II, 1920. The old school on Compton also served as a church before All Saints' Church was built to the design of the architect Norman Shaw in 1887.

Regent Street School. A Methodist establishment, this was first a Sunday School, run in conjunction with West Street until 1863, when it was run by a separate committee and became known as Brunswick School. It was a day school from 1840. In 1912 the headmaster was Mr H. Davis. Extensive additions were built in 1880 at a cost of £2,212, which was a considerable investment at the time. In 1912 there were 500 boys and girls and 135 infants on the role, and the average attendance was 360.

Regent Street School in about 1910. This group was photographed in the school yard, off Ball Haye Street. Miss Atkinson was the infants' mistress. The school has now been demolished.

Cheddleton School, class II, *c.* 1905. The headmaster for many years was Mr J.J. Parnell.

Leek Girls' High School, 1921.

Dame schools were a feature of education in Victorian and Edwardian England. Miss Milner's school, seen in this picture, catered for both girls and boys, and appears to have had a large number of teachers relative to the number of pupils.

Miss Marsland's school, Union Street, was a private school run under the auspices of the Congregational Church. Miss Gibson was in charge of the infants' section.

These happy children are seen at the end of Overton Bank, formerly known as Schoolings Bank. Behind the three adults the row of Quaker Cottages can be seen, and beyond is Sampson Salt's builder's yard.

The old Leek Grammar School on Clerk Bank was founded in 1723 by Thomas Parker, the 1st Earl of Macclesfield, who was born in Leek. For many years the headmaster was Mr John Sykes. The Sykes family were very prominent in education in Victorian Leek. In 1860 a Mr Joseph Sykes had a private school in Ball Haye Hall, and in 1868 the school was in Ford Street.

Leek High School in about 1901, photographed in the inner quadrangle behind the Nicholson Institute. The first headmaster of the school was Mr T.C. ('Toby') Warrington, who held the post for over thirty years.

# SECTION TWO

# The World of Work

A group of workers from Brough, Nicholson and Hall Ltd. Most of these men were joiners. Mr John Hall, a director of the company, often employed the firm's handymen on the maintenance and upkeep of 'John Hall's Gardens' at the rear of his home, Ball Haye Hall – now part of the park.

The knitting room at S. Mayers and Company's factory in Wellington Street, during the 1930s. This typical mill interior illustrates the labour-intensive nature of Leek's textile industry.

The Sander and Graf knitting room at Wardle and Davenport's factory, in the early 1930s. These German machines were widely used in Leek's textile mills.

The garter room at Clemesha Brothers and Birch Ltd, New Street, in about 1930. Leek's factories made a very wide range of textile products, garments and household goods.

Factory fires have always been a hazard in Leek's textile industry, where fine fibre dust and oil combined in a highly combustible fusion. This major fire at Brough, Nicholson and Hall Ltd occurred on 31 August 1915.

The aftermath of Brough's fire. The steel girders and pillars have been twisted into fantastic shapes by the intense heat. A group of local firemen survey the enormous damage.

These houses once stood next to the Nicholson Institute, in Stockwell Street. Demolition work appears to be under way prior to the building of the Technical Schools in 1899. One family, still in residence, has hung the washing out – almost as an act of defiance! The wide attic windows indicate the presence of weaving 'shades' on the top floor, where the residents would work their looms. Many of these 'shades' can still be seen around Leek, notably in King Street, Albion Street and London Street.

A group of workmen at Wall Grange Brickworks at about the turn of the century. The works closed in 1960, after a long and chequered history, when the kilns and workshops were demolished. The area has now been landscaped, and forms part of the Deep Haye Country Park.

Meakin's Smithy, Ashbourne Road. This old, stone-built forge stood opposite Moorhouse Street. With sleeves rolled up, these workmen are ready for the heavy work demanded by the farming industry.

Draymen with their loaded carts in Leek Market Place make a splendid picture as they stand with their heavy horses.

These Victorian firemen resemble a scene from an old silent comedy film. However, the captain, third from the left appears to have everything under control. The original Fire Engine House was on the old cattle market site, between the Talbot and the Cattle Market inns.

Robert Farrow (with the full white beard) was secretary of the fire brigade when this picture was taken in the late 1880s. Micah Carding was captain for a number of years. The horse-drawn fire engine was a 'Firefly Manual'. Robert Farrow was also the town's sanitary inspector during the 1880s and '90s. His reports present a revealing insight into the social conditions at that time.

In 1896 the new fire station at the top of Stockwell Street was built, the architect being Brealey. This picture was taken just prior to that event. Standing on the vehicle are, left to right: Eng. Carding, R. Carding, W. Wilshaw, 2nd Eng. Jones. On the ladder: H. Alcock (above), W. Davenport (below). Front row standing, left to right: H. Buxton, V. Carding, W. Wood, A. Carding, A.V. Holton, Lt. Clowes, Capt. Wardle, Capt. Carding, Dr. Hammersley, W.B. Nadin, T. Alcock, H. Billing.

This unusual vehicle was known as the 'Economic Hygienic Non-tipping House Refuse Vehicle'. It was designed by Mr Frank Green, Sanitary Inspector to Leek Urban District Council in 1929. He claimed that it had several revolutionary new features, such as easy low loading and automatic discharge. The Leek engineers, Charles Leek and Sons, were commissioned to manufacture a vehicle for the council's use, and Mr Green took out a patent on his invention.

Another council road vehicle, the steam road roller, is seen in this picture, on the Ashbourne Road below Lowe Hill.

The late afternoon sun lights up this scene in Cross Street. Brough, Nicholson and Hall's office and warehouse building on the left was connected to other departments of the factory by the covered wooden footbridge over the street. This stylish, curved frontage was the work of Sugden and Son, architects.

The shunting yard at Leek railway station, viewed from Barnfields Bridge in the late 1950s.

The remains of the canal basin at Leek, in the 1950s. The wharf-side buildings and sheds have been cleared. The canal was then filled in, and the area is now an industrial estate. Leek Gas Works stands in the left background.

# SECTION THREE
# Leisure and Sport

Leek Amateur Operatic Society's production of *H.M.S. Pinafore*, 1895. Members of the cast were, back row, left to right: J.G. Beckett, M. Prince, E. Challinor, V. Prince, S. Prince. Second row: Mrs Kineton Parkes, Miss Ada Allday, Kineton Parkes, W.E. Brindley. Front row: Miss Florence Parkes, Miss Lexy Munro. The society had a great reputation for producing Gilbert and Sullivan operettas with a high degree of skill. Kineton Parkes, a leading performer, was also Leek's librarian, and head of the School of Art. A man of many talents, he also wrote several novels.

Nine of the players in this photograph of Leek Football Club played in the famous match in the third round of the English Cup on 3 January 1885, when Leek lost to Queen's Park, Glasgow, by the narrow margin of 3–2 before a large crowd on the Westwood Lane ground. Knowles and Baskerville did not play in that match, but the team did include G.C. Wardle and J. Smethurst. The players in this picture are, back row, left to right: E. Hassall, F. Byrne, W. Knowles, H. Stonehewer, W. Allen. Front row, left to right: W. Vickerstaff, H.E. Whittles, A. Baskerville, G. Tudor, J. Brentnall, M. Rider.

This fine action shot of an incident in the Leek Combination Cup Final between St Mary's and Leek YMCA on 30 March 1907 was taken by W.H. Nithsdale. This keenly fought local match was watched by a large crowd, which included a number of ladies.

The Leek YMCA team which defeated St Mary's in the Leek Combination Cup, 1906/7. The players are, back row, left to right: G. Towers, A. Goodwin, H. Ellerton, G. Bagshaw. Middle row: A. Knight, H. Nichols, W. Bowyer, G.E. Plant. Front row: V. Finney, A. Bowyer, J. Smith, R. Carr, E. Ratcliffe. The picture also includes officials and the committee.

St Mary's football team in about 1920.

This picture shows a team of St Luke's Juniors, outside the Moss Rose. There was always a keen interest in local football at the beginning of this century, and many thrilling encounters were played between local teams before very large crowds. Teams from factories, clubs and churches were numerous.

Committee and players of Ball Haye Green FC, 1901/2. Ball Haye Green played on Isaac Bailey's field in Novi Lane, often before a crowd of over 2,000 spectators. The committee are, left to right: H. Wilson, J. Cottam, J. Perry, J. Smith, H. Biddulph, T.S. Myatt, D. Porter, C. Rhead, A. Green, G. Rider, G. Burnett, J. Day (secretary). The players are, back row: E. Tatton, F. Whitter, S. Ratcliffe, E. Shenton, J. Burnett, C. Ball, A. Nadin. Front row: F. Dale, A. Brown, R. Green, S. Pickford, E. Sherratt.

A Brough, Nicholson and Hall's works football team in the 1930s. Col. A.F. Nicholson is seated in the front row on the left.

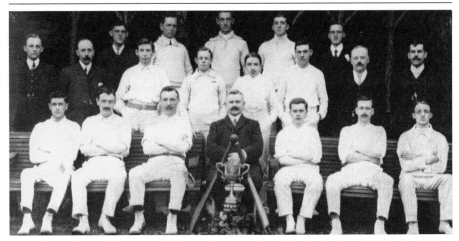

Brough's Cricket Club, 1913. This works team played in the Leek and District Cricket League, and were champions in 1911, 1912 and 1913. Back row includes, left to right: T. Beard, G. Bostock, C. Phillips, S. Goodwin. Middle row: J. Earls (secretary), H.H. Kirkham, H. Oliver, C. Hodgkinson, W.J. Roe, A. Fisher, R.H. Ball, A. Poyser. Front row: A. Yates, T. Sanders, J. Bentley, Mr W. Pickford (president), H. Cope, J. Hambleton, G. Tunnicliffe.

Leek Cyclists' Club, 1910. Back row, left to right: W. Howard, S. Godwin, W. Constantine, S. Newall, H. Smith, C. Simpson, H. Walters. Fourth row: T.W. Hawksworth, F. Salt, W.H. Capper, C. Pickford, J.J. Carding, F. Coates, H. Rigby, G.H. Wilson. Third row: B. Hill, J. Trafford, H. Cater, A. Armitt, C. Brassington, H. Kirkham, W.H. Robinson, J. Fowler, G.H. Pickford. Second row: A.J. Hall, J. Wilkinson, G. Watson, G. Beswick, R.A. Crombie, T. Beswick, W.H. Hill, R. Manuell, E. Trafford, G.W. Cook. Front row: J. Hudson, T. Messham, A. Barnett, W. Kinsey, T.S. Myatt, C. Heath, W.T. Cook, J.P. Fellowes-Smith, A. Billington, S. Taylor.

This photograph of members of Leek Fishing Club was taken in the early 1900s. Front row, left to right: John Pickford, Master Horne, Charlie Bowcock, Samuel Goldstraw, Master Bowcock. Second row: William Hall, James Creathorne, Sam Clark, William Horne, Robert Hill, Tom Taylor, John Hurst, John Ind, Henry Prime, Master Prime. Third row: John Goodwin, John Astles, John Rushton, Gus Bayley, Jock Rider, Roland Rider, Albert Rex, Tom Nightingale, Thomas Taylor sen.

One of the pleasures of the past, before people had their own transport, was a coach outing in an open-topped charabanc. Here, the *Moorland Queen* is carrying a happy company of Leek trippers for a day in the countryside, or at the seaside. The North Wales coastal resorts were always a popular venue.

Shopkeepers, too, had their day out. The traditional 'traders outing' continued into the 1950s. On one Thursday during the summer all Leek shops closed for the day to allow the shopkeepers a day out. On this occasion, during the 1930s, the traders enjoyed a cruise on the River Thames.

The Leek Temperance Prize Band, 1901. Leek has always had a great musical tradition, and brass bands were always in demand for concerts and processions.

A unique event – a live performing bear in Derby Street. Although the street appears to be deserted, great numbers turned out to witness the performance, but the crowds kept a safe distance. They are gathered around the Ball Haye Street corner, in the background.

The horse-drawn Leek to Buxton coach is seen here taking on passengers outside the Duke of York inn, Derby Street. A strong team of horses was necessary to tackle the challenging hills on this journey.

Leek Methodists have always enjoyed their choirs, performing the classic choral works with great skill. In this picture of the Mount Pleasant Choir, the organist, Mr H. Ball, is seated in the centre of the front row.

Mr Ball is seen here again with the Mount Pleasant Choir.

The gentry and nobility usually travelled by their own private coach, complete with staff and liveried attendants. This is a scene of bustle and activity outside the Red Lion in Leek Market Place, as the requirements of the Earl of Shrewsbury are attended to.

This gentle scene was captured in Leek Market Place, outside the Red Lion, as a gentleman arrives at the hotel by pony and trap.

Outside the Moss Rose inn, Buxton Road, on the very edge of town. This photograph shows a country family stopping, perhaps for refreshment, before continuing on their journey into the moorlands.

The rambling section of the sports club which met at the Mechanics Institute is seen here in the Manifold Valley in 1926. Mr Arthur Ratcliffe, MP for Leek, is standing on the extreme left of the picture.

# SECTION FOUR

# Yesterday's Shops and Market Days

The name of Fallon in Leek is synonymous with poultry, fruit and greengroceries. The old-established business of J. Fallon and Co., fruiterers and fishmongers, was trading on this site, 8 Stockwell Street, in 1884.

In the same line of business, W. Fallon and Co. had this shop in St Edward Street in the late Victorian years. It stood next to the Globe Yard and the shop of Shallcross, where a favourite Leek delicacy, twisted sticks of sticky toffee, was sold. These buildings were demolished when High Street was constructed.

In the days before refrigeration and frozen foods, this is how W. Fallon and Sons displayed their goods at 14 Derby Street. Poultry and rabbits festoon the entire shop frontage. Mr Fallon and his staff stand in the doorways, and the delivery boys' cycles are parked by the kerb, ready for an instant delivery to any address in the district.

Four smart waitresses in their starched white aprons and caps outside the White Hart Restaurant, in Stockwell Street. A popular refreshment stop for passing travellers, particularly cyclists, the restaurant served high quality teas and grills.

Harrod's store – Leek! Situated at the corner of Dog Lane and Stanley Street, this shop with a famous name sold pots, pans, baskets and a wide range of household goods.

A shopkeeper by the splendid name of Sly once occupied this little shop at 47 Derby Street. A boot and shoe shop, it was packed with footwear of every kind.

Posed outside Mr Sly's shoe shop, this old Leek cobbler and bootmaker makes a splendid character study.

A window display packed with Christmas fare in the Maypole grocery shop at 31 Derby Street. The all-male staff, smartly turned out in their clean white aprons, pose for the camera.

This was the grocer's shop of Arthur Hay and Sons at 57 Derby Street in 1900. Mr Hay also had a shop at 45 West Street.

This spick-and-span delivery cart and well-groomed horse owned by T. Burgess, baker and confectioner, of 12 St Edward Street, was a familiar sight as it made deliveries around Leek during the Edwardian years.

Everett's well-stocked cycle store stood at the corner of Brook Street and Pickwood Road, now the entrance to a car park. The earlier name for Pickwood Road was 'Backsides'.

Bradley's, gents' and boys' outfitters, occupied this shop at 29 Market Place for over twenty-five years. By 1928, when this property on the north west corner of the Market Place was demolished, they had moved to 5 Stanley Street.

Thomas Mark was a bookseller, stationer and printer at 6 Derby Street in the 1890s. He kept a very wide range of stationery products, and also published an almanac which included much useful local information.

The traditional Wednesday market. Leek's ancient Market Charter was granted in the reign of King John. When this photograph was taken in about 1890, the block of property at the north-west corner of the Market Place was occupied by Robert West, clock and watchmaker, who was responsible for the installation in 1883 of the large public clock on the wall, which can just be seen at the top of the picture.

This scene of bustling activity is Leek cattle market in about 1910, when the farmer's mode of transport was usually a horse and cart.

The cattle market on its original Smithfield site had some fine beasts for sale when this picture was taken. This misty Edwardian scene, with Haywood Street in the background, perfectly captures the atmosphere of this weekly market.

This deserted and ice-bound view of the cattle market is in sharp contrast to the usual Wednesday scene when the market would be thronged with farmers, dealers, auctioneers and drovers. In the background can be seen the Smithfield Commercial Restaurant, or 'Coffee Tavern' and the row of Smithfield Cottages. The area is now the site of the bus station and its surrounding shops.

Another brief moment in time is caught by the camera of W.H. Nithsdale. He titles this picture, 'Pleased to meet you', and it depicts two people from the moorlands exchanging greetings, and no doubt the odd bit of gossip, on their regular Wednesday visit to Leek market.

# SECTION FIVE

# Town Scenes our Grandparents Knew

A fine view of Derby Street in about 1910. Skinner and Son, the ironmongers and hardware store on the left, was founded in 1894 and is still trading today.

Leek's old public baths can be seen on the left of this picture, *c.* 1900. The small building with the pyramid-shaped roof housed a public weighing machine. It stood on the area known as 'Sparrow Park', part of the old cattle market site before the Monument was built.

Sanders' Buildings, at the corner of Derby Street and Haywood Street, was designed by Sugden and Son, the Leek architects, in 1894 as shops with living accommodation. It is still known locally as 'Mears's Corner', from the name of a former shopkeeper.

This scene is now dominated by the Nicholson War Memorial, or 'Monument', and the traffic island. The old cattle market extended into this area, which is bounded by Cawdry Buildings, Fountain Street, the Cattle Market Inn and the Talbot Hotel. In the background are St Luke's Church, the Fountain Street Primitive Methodist Chapel and Brough, Nicholson and Hall's factory, with its tall chimney.

There were apparently no parking restrictions in Derby Street when this picture was taken in the late Victorian years. The inn on the left, with its hanging sign and shops on either side, was the Dog and Partridge.

St Edward Street is lined with buildings of differing style, age and character. There is no uniformity and no straight lines, but nevertheless there is great harmony. St Edward Street has a number of fine houses which were once the homes of many of Leek's prominent citizens.

One such house was Spout Hall, part of which can be seen on the extreme left of the picture. This impressive Victorian building was designed by the architect Norman Shaw for Hugh Sleigh.

St Edward Street looking towards Compton and St Mary's Church. The larger house on the left was owned in turn by Stephen Goodwin and Andrew Jukes Worthington – local silk manufacturers. The Georgian building on the right was the town house of Sir Thomas Wardle.

Stanley Street at around the turn of the century.

A well-earned feed was the reward for this horse after a busy day of deliveries. The scene is Cruso's Yard, with Stockwell Street in the background.

This picture of Broad Street shows the builder's yard of Thomas Grace on the right, with a row of typical weavers' cottages on the left.

Buxton Road. This early view of what is now a very busy road junction shows Abbotts Road, formerly Abbotts Lane, leading off to the left.

Ashbourne Road. The row of fine Victorian town houses on the right were desirable properties on the edge of town.

The extremely tall chimney of Stephen Goodwin and Tatton's factory dominates this view of the top of Mill Street. The factory was burned down during the 1940s. On the extreme right is the old drinking fountain in the wall of St Edward's churchyard.

Mill Street, Leek, in the late Victorian years.

These old properties were typical of the houses on Mill Street, many of which stood three or four storeys high. The tightly knit community was virtually self-contained, having its own shops, pubs, schools and churches.

The Methodist Chapel and Ragged School are on the extreme right of this picture. Above this, and towering over the houses, is 'Big Mill', built originally by Sugden and Son for the textile firm of Lovatt and Gould in 1860. From 1896 it became Wardle and Davenport Ltd, providing employment for many people living in the area.

This picture of the lower end of Mill Street, with some local children walking home, shows the row of trees which added a touch of greenery to an otherwise industrial scene.

# SECTION SIX

# On Parade

Processions have always been a feature of life in Leek. The annual Sunday School festival, or 'Club Day', still takes place on the third Saturday in July of each year. In this picture a junior band leads a Sunday School contingent down Stockwell Street. The festival, formerly known as 'cap Sunday', started in the early 1800s.

The Sunday Schools are seen here assembling in the Market Place for the traditional short service during the 1890s.

The Sunday School festival procession of 1910 is seen here in Church Street.

A feature of the Sunday School festival has always been the assembly in the Market Place, where hymns are sung. This typical scene of around the turn of the century shows, above the heads of the crowd, the eastern side of the market square, with the Cock Inn, the Red Lion and the Butter Market.

A Sunday School procession makes its way up the cobbled St Edward Street, with St Mary's Roman Catholic Church in the background.

Crowds of spectators throng the pavements and spill into the road as the Sunday School procession proceeds along Stockwell Street. These pretty Edwardian girls wear their charming hats and white dresses with pride.

Adult church members usually turn out to support the children on Club Day. These ladies from Brunswick Methodist Church are seen here dressed in the fashions of the 1930s.

Club Day, 1929. Children from St Luke's Sunday School enter the Market Place, with their banner. The gentleman on the right is Mr Charles Hurd, school attendance officer.

Club Day, 1933. A group of children from Bethesda Methodist Church have assembled in the Market Place, with their maypole, ready for the hymn singing.

The traditional scene in the Market Place will be familiar to anyone who has memories of their Sunday School days. This Club Day, in the late 1930s, has Mr F. Whitter as the conductor, and the British Legion band accompanying the singing.

A mixture of shyness and excitement is seen on the faces of these children, assembled in the Market Place in 1934.

Baskets of flowers, maypoles, ribbons, white dresses and banners are the hallmarks of Club Day.

It is often difficult to distinguish between Club Day and Band of Hope photographs, but the predominance of young adults in this procession in St Edward Street suggests that it is probably the Band of Hope.

Another annual church procession around the streets of Leek, on similar lines to Club Day, was the Band of Hope demonstration. This organization was allied to the temperance movement, and also assembled in the Market Place for a short service.

The Band of Hope procession of 29 June 1907 proceeds along Stockwell Street, with the West Street banner carried aloft.

Royal occasions have always inspired a procession in Leek. The coronation festival procession of 1911 makes its way up Church Street, giving the spectators lining Overton Bank a splendid view.

Crowds assemble in the Market Place for the 1911 coronation celebrations.

Leek coronation celebrations, 22 June 1911. The West Street Methodist Sunday School banner is seen passing Greystones in Stockwell Street. These colourful banners were beautifully produced in silks and woven fabrics and were always carried with pride in the various processions.

Boy Scouts in their traditional uniforms are seen accompanying St Edward's Parish Church in the 1911 coronation procession in Stockwell Street.

Large crowds also turned out to witness the Trades Demonstration on 22 June 1907.

The Leek Volunteer Band parades down Ashbourne Road. The band played regularly at open air concerts in the Market Place during the early 1900s, and was always in demand for parades. The Talbot Hotel is on the left of the picture and the Coffee Tavern on the right.

August 1914. This was the scene at the top of West Street as the old Leek Battery wheels round the corner. Led by Major (later Colonel) Challinor, they are leaving the barracks at the start of the First World War. The crowds turned out to give them a rousing send-off, unaware of the enormous scale of the carnage in the conflict ahead.

A last goodbye. An officer pauses on the Ashbourne Road, just beyond Lowe Hill, to say farewell to a group of Leek ladies and children, as the Leek Battery marches off to war in August 1914.

The parade to celebrate the peace following the First World War turns out of Shirburn Road into Ashbourne Road, led by Boy Scouts and the fire brigade.

Another view of the same parade, with a brass band leading a contingent of soldiers.

Following the First World War a carnival was held at Ball Haye Green to raise money to provide a suitable war memorial for the area. In this picture, one of the floats reflects the victory theme.

A float in the Ball Haye Green carnival pauses in front of the Co-op cottages.

The carnival procession assembles in the Market Place.

# SECTION SEVEN

# Civic and Public
# Events

LAYING THE FOUNDATION STONES,
MILL ST WESLEYAN SUNDAY SCHOOL, AUG 17.

The laying of the foundation stone at Mill Street Ragged School. This Methodist school was built in 1870 and catered for 165 children from the large families living in Mill Street at that time. The average attendance recorded at the school in 1912 was only 59 – an indication of the high level of childhood illnesses and other social factors prevailing at the time.

An Edwardian missionary fund-raising event with stalls in the Market Place is here drawing some support from the people of Leek.

An election meeting outside the Coffee Tavern in 1910. The Liberal candidate, Robert Pearce, is addressing the crowd. Among those on the platform with him are A.H. Moore and R.S. Milner.

The general election of 1910 is again featured in this photograph, but this time the Conservative candidate, Colonel Bromley Davenport, is on the platform. In this second election of 1910, Robert Pearce was elected by a narrow margin.

This was the scene on 20 August 1925, at the unveiling and dedication of the Nicholson War Memorial. Civic, church and military dignitaries are assembled for the start of the ceremony.

The memorial tablet has now been unveiled by Lt.-Gen. Sir Charles Harrington, GBE, KCB, DSO (GOC Northern Command), and dedicated by the Bishop of Stafford. The impressive memorial was presented to the town by Sir Arthur and Lady Nicholson in memory of their son Lt. Basil Lee Nicholson and other local men who died in the First World War. Built of Portland Stone, it stands 90 ft high and was designed by Thomas Worthington and Sons of Manchester.

Chairman's Sunday, 1934. Leek Urban District councillors and officials, elegantly attired, are seen in their annual church parade. The chairman on this occasion was Councillor Fred Hill.

During his year of office, Councillor Hill performed many civic duties. Here he is addressing the assembly at the building of the new Salvation Army citadel in Salisbury Street.

W.H. Nithsdale has captured this illustration of a worthy social service in Edwardian Leek, when the poorer children of the town were provided with a nourishing hot dinner in the Butter Market Hall.

This group of veterans of the First World War represented the Leek branch of the British Legion at the Royal Review in Hyde Park in 1937.

The strength of Methodism in Leek is illustrated by this large group of men who attended the men's Bible class at West Street School. The photograph was taken on Coronation Day, 22 June 1911. Back row, left to right: W. Osborne, J. Brisley, C. Sherratt, G. Pickering, W.H. Pickering, T. Hunt, J.A. Vigrass, H.H. Goodwin, H. Rhead, T. Vigrass, H. Rushton, H. Brentnall, T. Higginbotham, G. Crombie, W. Vaughan, T. Burgess, H. Morton, A. Nixon. Third row (standing): A. Hunt, A. Bayley, H. Bayley, F. Goodwin, J. Bonsall, T. Bloor, S. Bayley, F. Kelsall, A.J. Kent, D. Ingham, A. Prime, J. Loxley, J. Hall (supt.), J. Wood, H. Morriss, J. Morriss, W. Morriss, A. Leadbeater, J. Bayley, J. Swindlehurst, H. Ralphs, A.J. Hine, G. Hulme, H. Brocklehurst, H. Bayley, E. Fernyhough, W. Marren, B. Farrall. Second row (sitting): J. Bayley, W. Ward, J. Morrow, H. Lomas, A. Gibson, D. Lovatt, T. Goodwin (teacher), L. Ball, L. Ball, J. Gaunt, S. Murray, G. Stonier, S. Goodwin, A. Leadbeater. Front row: F. Gosling, F. Owen, W. Turner, W. Ball, W. Brentnall, S. Owen, T. Wardle, A. Worthington, W. Rhead, E. Matthews, W. Hudson.

This and the following four pictures are all parts of the same large panoramic photograph of a crowded event in Leek Market Place. Here, in the foreground, the local fire brigade keep a watchful eye on the proceedings from their horse-drawn vehicle.

This longer view over the heads of the crowd shows people on the balconies and rooftops on the left. The block of property at the north-west corner of the Market Place is clearly shown, here occupied by Hilton's, with Robert West's large public clock on the wall.

Flags and bunting are strung across the width of the Market Place and around the splendid Victorian street lamp in the centre. The Georgian frontage of Foxlowe dominates the north side of the square. When it was the home of Mr and Mrs John Cruso during the late Victorian years its address was commonly known as 'No.1, Leek', in deference to Mrs Cruso, who was a great public benefactor and held in very high esteem by the people of Leek.

The dense crowd massed in the square is a clear indication that a public event of some importance is taking place. A group of civic leaders are seen on an elevated platform at the top of the picture. What, then, is the event?

This view of the eastern side of the Market Place provides the clue. The scaffolding on
he right indicates that the Butter Market is under construction, which fixes the date as
887. The national flags which mingle with the various church banners suggest that this
s Queen Victoria's Jubilee celebration.

# Homage to Royalty

This was the scene on the Roches on the occasion of the visit of HRH Princess Mary of Cambridge, cousin of Queen Victoria, and Prince Teck on 23 August 1872. The 'Queen's Chair', cut out of the rock, is on the right just above the sheer drop.

The royal party and local dignitaries on the Roches, 23 August 1872. Included in this group are the Duchess of Teck, the Countess of Shrewsbury, the Duke of Teck, Mr P.L. Brocklehurst of Swythamley Hall, and the Earl of Shrewsbury.

Queen Victoria's Jubilee, 21 June 1887. It was a very hot day and the forest of umbrellas provided shelter from the sun. This crowded scene has an interesting background, dominated by the fine Victorian frontage of the Talbot Hotel. To the right is the row of weavers' cottages at the bottom of Ashbourne Road, next to the White Lion, with the Coffee Tavern on the extreme right.

The old Leek Grammar School on Clerk Bank was decorated for the Royal Jubilee celebrations, 1887. The headmaster, Mr J. Sykes, with the beard, is standing in the centre, with Mr J.J.T. Sykes to his right.

A crowd of prominent Leek citizens is assembled outside the Conservative Club in Church Street, decorated for Queen Victoria's Jubilee, 27 June 1887.

Weddings of members of the royal family have also inspired Leek people to mount a parade. St Edward Street was in festive spirit on 6 July 1893 for the celebration of the marriage of Princess Mary to the Duke of York.

For Queen Victoria's Diamond Jubilee in 1897 Leek streets were decorated with a series of arches bedecked with flowers and foliage. This was the arch at the bottom of St Edward Street.

The festive arch at the bottom of Mill Street had an agricultural theme.

This arch was erected at the junction of Park Road and Buxton Road to welcome the Duke and Duchess of York on their visit to Leek, 28 July 1900. Victoria Mill, the house and the cottages around the corner have all been demolished, and a health centre now stands on the site.

The royal visit, 1900. This solidly constructed arch stood at the top of Stockwell Street, near the old fire station.

The royal visit, 1900. This arch in Market Street frames the Nicholson Institute in the background.

Stockwell Street was an impressive sight on 28 July 1900 when the Duke and Duchess of York visited Leek to open the new Technical Schools.

'Success to the School' proclaims this substantial arch in St Edward Street, erected for the visit of the Duke and Duchess of York in 1900.

The royal visit, 1900. The procession of carriages, with the Duke and Duchess of York, is seen here entering St Edward Street.

The royal visitors toured Brough, Nicholson and Hall's factory during their visit to Leek. This brochure was produced to celebrate the occasion. In 1913 they returned to Leek, as King George V and Queen Mary, and toured the same factory.

This was the scene on 28 July 1900, when the Duchess of York opened the new Technical Schools (now Leek College of Further Education). The duke also had a part to play – he laid the foundation stone of the nearby Carr Gymnasium.

The Proclamation of George V is read on 11 May 1910 outside the Town Hall in Market Street by Mr J.H. Bishton, chairman of Leek Urban District Council.

The parade enters the Market Place for the second reading of the Proclamation of George V . . .

. . . and this was the assembly in the Market Place for that proclamation. It also happened to be market day.

The 1911 coronation procession was a great occasion for Leek and large crowds lined the street. Here in Derby Street the parade passes in front of the old public baths.

For the royal visit of George V and Queen Mary on 23 April 1913 many triumphal arches were erected around the town. This one, in Broad Street, was designed by Jack Ratcliffe for the National Reservists.

# Rudyard

The Jubilee Stone at Rudyard. This rough-hewn block of local stone was erected by the parishioners of Horton to commemorate Queen Victoria's Diamond Jubilee, 1897. Many other significant dates have been added since then, and the stone has become a potted history of the twentieth century to date.

This picture of the road through Rudyard village shows the impressive Victorian houses on the right. These are more typical of town houses than village ones, but this reflects the ambience of the area. They are an indication of the prosperity brought to Rudyard in its heyday as a pleasure resort.

Rudyard village at the turn of the century.

This charming, peaceful scene in the woods at Rudyard is one of local photographer George Hill's 'Penny Postcards' series. It was postmarked 1911 and the sender, who was clearly not enjoying good weather, writes: 'Raining hard and generally rotten. May the Lord preserve me from another holiday in the Potteries.'

Woodside Pavilion and Tea Gardens, Rudyard. These tea rooms, with their verandas of flowers and plants and gently sloping lawns were a feature of Rudyard in its heyday.

A vanished age of Edwardian gentility is evoked by this peaceful view of the Woodside Pavilion and Tea Gardens at Rudyard.

The dam at the head of Rudyard Lake provided a promenade overlooking the water. A roller-skating rink and other entertainments operated here, adding to the attractions of Rudyard for visitors. On 25 June 1877 a 'Grand Aquatic Entertainment' is reputed to have attracted around 20,000 visitors. A variety of water sports took place, and the advertising stressed that 'the bathing costumes, being full and complete, the most fastidious of either sex may, with propriety, be present at this Entertainment'.

The lakeside at Rudyard, 1910. The lake was authorized by an Act of Parliament in 1797 to provide a water supply for the canal. Pleasure boating has always been a great attraction, and continues to be so.

A day out at Rudyard was always a great treat for local families, and the crowds were often increased by visitors from much further afield, who travelled by excursion train and coach.

Rudyard Lake, 1910, in its heyday as a pleasure resort and Edwardian playground. In the early summer of 1863 John Lockwood Kipling, a pottery designer from Burslem, met Alice Macdonald at a picnic party at the lake. The place clearly made a great impression on the couple. They subsequently married and immediately sailed for India where their first child was born in Bombay on 30 December 1865. He was named Rudyard, thus perpetuating in the annals of English literature the name of the place where his parents first met.

Boating on the lake at Rudyard has always been a favourite leisure activity. This typical Edwardian scene shows a group of fashionably dressed visitors enjoying their day out.

Passenger boats on the lake at Rudyard. With its gently sloping, deeply wooded banks, the lake is a very attractive sailing venue.

A busy scene on the lakeside at Rudyard. A large steam boat was once a very popular attraction for visitors.

An early advertising card, dated 1907, in which an agricultural merchant graphically illustrates the advantages of potash salts. The card proclaims: 'Swedes at Rudyard Green. Gain from 1 cwt. sulphate of potash : 7 tons 11¾ cwt. of swedes.'

Reproduced here is a card advertising the open-air swimming pool at Freshwater, on the main Macclesfield Road just beyond Rudyard. This was a popular, lively spot much favoured by the young people of Leek.

# SECTION TEN

# Out of Town

Upperhulme was described by W.H. Nithsdale in his book *In the Highlands of Staffordshire* as '. . . nestling Swiss-like beneath these formidable Rocks and Roches'. William Tatton's original dye works, founded in 1869 in the old water-powered flax mill, is to the left of the picture. There was a fire here in 1891.

These fine old stone cottages at Upperhulme once housed workers at the nearby Tatton's dye works.

These children are walking along the main Leek to Buxton road, in the shadow of Ramshaw Rocks, an outcrop of Millstone Grit which provides a spectacular backdrop to this photograph, taken in about 1905.

The roots of Methodism at Flash go back to 1773, the time of John Wesley. Two brothers, George and James Redfern, were pioneers of the work at this time, and this fine chapel was built in 1784. It was enlarged in 1821 to accommodate the growing congregation of quarryworkers and miners in the area, to become one of the largest chapels in the district. It is now closed.

Warslow post office, c. 1900. The post office also served this moorland community as a general store with groceries and provisions, drapery and household goods being generally available.

A quiet corner of Warslow village.

This peaceful scene on the Leek Canal shows the canal-side cottage on the right (now demolished) which stood at the junction with the Leek arm of the canal.

The camera of W.H. Nithsdale has captured this busy scene on the Caldon Canal at Cheddleton, *c.* 1904.

The main road through Wetley Rocks in about 1905. W.H. Nithsdale's photograph has recorded the older part of the village, with the wheelwright's shop in the centre, behind the cart. The old chapel was to the left, behind the stone wall.

Wetley Rocks, 1900. The inn on the right, now the Powys Arms, was formerly known as the Arblasters Arms, a name which commemorated a former Lord of the Manor. On the left, another inn, the Mason's Arms, stood on the site of the present petrol station.

The Avenue, Wetley Rocks. This stretch of the busy main road is very different now, and is no longer lined with trees.

A quiet road at Longsdon, *c.* 1905. The sender of this postcard was clearly something of a romantic, for he writes, to a young lady, 'Is not this a nice bungalow for two?' The end of the story is not known!

The well-dressing queen and her attendants are seen here in procession at the traditional Endon well-dressing festival, 1916.

Endon village, *c.* 1910. Beyond the ford, on the left, stand some old stone cottages which have had extensions added. On the right is the former Methodist Chapel and Sunday School, built in 1835 at a cost of £217. It was later converted into a dwelling house when the new chapel was built near the Fountain.

The well at Endon, which is decorated at the annual well-dressing festival, was given to the village in 1845 by Thomas Heaton, a local landowner.

Cyclists have called at the old post office in the centre of Meerbrook village. The old school building is seen on the left, and in the background, centre, is the Three Horse Shoes Inn, bearing the same name as another hostelry about a mile away on the main Buxton road.

These Edwardian young ladies appear to be having some difficulty with their punt on the canal feeder near Rushton.

The level-crossing at Rushton, in the days of the railway. Rushton was an important station on the Churnet Valley line, and the station house and buildings are examples of the fine railway architecture which typified the North Staffordshire Railway.

W.H. Nithsdale's picture of the well-dressing ceremony at Rushton is dated 1907. This ancient tradition, usually associated with Derbyshire, was carried on at Rushton for many years, but has now ceased. St Helen's Well, near the church, was dressed annually with flowers, leaves, moss and foliage in the traditional manner.

Rushton well-dressing, 1912. A group of officials and village worthies, the ladies wearing splendid hats, are assembled outside the marquee.

The fish ladders on the River Dane at Danebridge.

A quiet corner of the Dane Valley at Danebridge. This footbridge provided access to some splendid walking country.

Travelling on foot is often the only way to traverse the moorlands in the depth of winter. Here a solitary figure is seen walking towards Leek through Solomon's Hollow on the Buxton road.

A farmer struggles home through the deep snow on Thorncliffe Bank – an area frequently swept by blizzards which render these roads impassable, often for long periods.

# Acknowledgements

This book has been compiled from photographs in my collection which have been acquired from various sources – some purchased, some loaned, some kindly given to me. A number of people, therefore, should be thanked, for without their generosity my collection would be poor indeed.

I should name, first of all, fellow collectors George Bowyer and Geoffrey Fisher, who have frequently shared their finds with me, and given me many useful clues about problem pictures.

In addition, I wish to thank the following sources:

Leek Public Library • *Leek News* • Miss M. Hudson • Miss Wardle
Mrs Whitter • Mr R. Milner • Mr R. Buxton • Mr Pedlar • Mr J. Felthouse
Miss J. Forrester • Mrs Stretch • Mr Sheldon • Mr Wheeldon • Mrs Dale
Mrs Gibson • Mrs Langham • Mr G. Short • Mr D. Mycock
Mr R.G. Wragg • Mr S. Hobson • Miss P. Starling • Mr B. Turner
Mrs Johnson • Mr P. Anderton • Mr B. Jeuda • Mr P. Poole • Mrs C. Walton
Leek Historical Society • Leek Field Club. With the generosity of so many people, it is inevitable that there will be omissions to this list, and if this is so, I apologize unreservedly.

I must also commend those countless Leek people whose old photographs regularly appear in the 'Down Memory Lane' feature in the *Leek Post and Times*. I frequently see pictures here which I have not got, but they are always an inspiration to me, and it is good to see that these old photographs are cherished and preserved. Their value is inestimable.

Finally I must thank my wife, who frequently wonders where in our home my vast collection of material is to be stored, but usually accepts the inevitable when I claim the odd corner or two. Her patience and understanding are much appreciated.